MUSIC OF THE WORLD

TEXT BY:
ANDREA BERGAMINI
ILLUSTRATIONS BY:
STUDIO L. R. GALANTE, MANUELA CAPPON, L. R. GALANTE,
ALESSANDRO MENCHI, FRANCESCO SPADONI

BARRON'S

DoGi

English translation ©
Copyright 1999
by Barron's Educational
Series, Inc.
Original edition © 1998 by
DoGi spa, Florence Italy
Title of original edition:
*Civiltà musicali: suoni e
colori dei popoli nel mondo*
Italian edition by:
Andrea Bergamini
Graphic Display:
Sebastiano Ranchetti
Illustrations:
Studio L. R. Galante
Manuela Cappon
L. R. Galante
Alessandro Menchi
Francesco Spadoni
Art director:
Sebastiano Ranchetti
Page make-up:
Sebastiano Ranchetti
Katherine Carson Forden
Iconographic researcher:
Katherine Carson Forden
Editorial Staff:
Andrea Bachini
Francesco Milo
Translation from Italian by:
Anna Maria Salmeri Pherson

HOW TO READ THIS BOOK

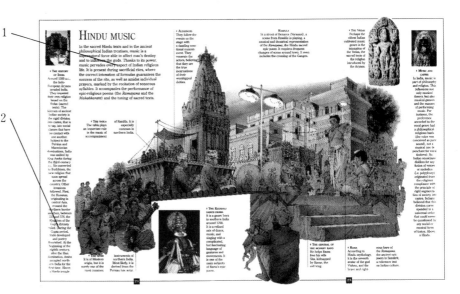

Every facing page is a chapter on the different musical traditions of the world and on the political-military, economic, or ethnic history of the multitudes of human civilizations that have originated them. The text above on the left (1) and the large illustration in the middle deal with the main subject. The small side-columns (2) provide the historical, ethnic, and religious background. The other elements of the page—photos, reproductions of prints of the time, and portraits—complement the information.

ACKNOWLEDGMENTS

ABBREVIATIONS: *t:* (top) / *b:* (below) / *c:* (center) / *r:* (right) / *l:* (left)

ILLUSTRATIONS:
The illustrations displayed in this volume are new and original. They have been created by DoGi s.r.l., which owns the copyright.

SPECIFIC CREDITS: Alessandro Bartolozzi: 15 t; Manuela Cappon: 18–19, 26–27, 30–31, 38–39, 40–41, 42–43; L. R. Galante: 10–11, 14–15, 20–21, 28–29, 46–47, 50–51, 54–55, 56–57; Alessandro Menchi: 12–13, 24–25, 32–33, 34–35, 52–53,. 62–63; Sergio: 18 t; Andrea Ricciardi: 48–49, 58–59; Francesco Spadoni: 6–7, 8–9, 16–17, 22–23, 36–37, 44–45, 60–61.

TITLE PAGE: Alessandro Menchi

COVER: L. R. Galante

LIST OF REPRODUCTIONS:
DoGi s.r.l. has done its best to discover possible rights of third parties. We apologize for any omissions or mistakes that might have occurred, and we will be pleased to introduce the appropriate corrections in later editions of this book. (The works reproduced in their totality are followed by the letter a (all); those partially reproduced are followed by the letter d (detail).

6 *Aborigines* (K&B, FLORENCE/R.ROSSI) a; **7** *Curt Sachs* (ARCHIVIO DOGI, FLORENCE) a; **8l** *Single-headed barrel drum from Ghana*, height 27³/₄ in (70.5 cm), diameter 9³/₅ in (24.5 cm) (ASHANTI, GHANA); **8r** *A gathering of chiefs in a Griot settlement in Senegambia* (ARCHIVIO DOGI, FLORENCE) a; **9b** *Bantu Mangebetu slit drum* (MUSEO NAZIONALE DI ANTROPOLOGIA E ETNOLOGIC/FLORENCE/G. VALSECCHI) a; **9t** *Man of the Masai tribe* (K&B, FLORENCE/V. CAVIRINI) a; **10** George Catlin, *Games of the Choctaw*, painting (NATIONAL GALLERY OF ART, WASHINGTON, D.C.) d; **11l** *Jim Morrison* (REDFERNS,

LONDON/CHUCK BOYD) d; **11r** Howard Terpning, *A Cheyenne man of medicine* (THE GREENWICH WORKSHOP, INC.) d; **11b** Elliott and Fry, *Black Elk with his father* (SMITHSONIAN INSTITUTION, WASHINGTON, D.C.) a; **12** *Maori's Haka dance* (NEW ZEALAND EMBASSY PHOTO); **13** *Girl of Tuvalu* (AGENZIA CONTRASTO, ROME) a; **14** *Royal board game of the 24 squares of Ur* (BRITISH MUSEUM, LONDON/ERICH LESSING/AGENZIA CONTRASTO) d; **16** *Nefertiti* (MUSEO ARCHEOLOGICO, FLORENCE); **17** *The Vintage,* Tomb of Minnakht, Sheikh Abd el-Qurna, 18th dynasty (WERNER FORMAN) a; **19** *Synagogue,* Florence (K&B, FLORENCE/G. VALSECCHI) a; **20** *Parthenon,* Athens (K&B, FLORENCE/G. VALSECCHI) a; **21l** *Cover of the English edition of Odyssey* (ARCHIVIO L. GALANTE/PHOTO SERGE DOMINGIE/MARCO RABATTI) a; **21r** Raphael, *School of Athens,* 1509–1510, fresco, base 303 in (770 cm) (VATICAN MUSEUMS) d; **22** *The Chinese Great Wall* (K&B, FLORENCE/A. VERGARI) d; **23l** Wu Daozi, *Confucius,* Paper reproduction of an engraving by rubbing technique (IGDA, MILAN) a; **23r** *Musician,* T'ang Dynasty, terracotta (MUSÉE GUIMET, PARIS/ERICH LESSING/AGENZIA CONTRASTO) d; **24t** *A Jain Temple* at Lodruva, Rajasthan, India (K&B, FLORENCE/F. PORCINAI) a; **24b** *Kathakali dance* (PANKAJ SHAH, BOMBAY) d; **25f** *The Sun,* one of the main deities of the Vedas (SURYA SCULPTURE, MUSEUM OF LUCKNOW) a; **25r** *A Sadhu Man,* India (K&B, FLORENCE/F. PORCINAI) d; **26** *Kakogenzai Ingakyo, A Sutra text,* Nara Period, ink and color on paper (HOONIN OF DAIGO-JI, KYOTO, JAPAN) d; **27** Anonymous, *A Shinto Deity,* Heian period, painted wood (MATSUNO-O JINJIA, KYOTO); **28** *Arabs at battle* (ARCHIVIO DOGI, FLORENCE) d; **28b** *Pilgrims going to Mecca,* Monte Rahma (ABBAS/MAGNUM/AGENZIA CONTRASTO,

ROME) a; **29** *The Great Mosque of Cordoba* (ARCHIVIO DOGI, FLORENCE) a; **30** *Miniature of a Chorale* (MUSEO CIVICO, BOLOGNA) a; **31l** *Minnesinger Heinrich von Meissen with troubadours,* c.1320, manuscript (PRIVATE COLLECTION) d; **31c** *The Guidonian Hand* (MUSEO TEATRALE ALLA SCALA, MILAN) a; **31r** *Nave of the Cathedral of Bourges,* c. 1195–1245 (ARCHIVIO DOGI, FLORENCE) a; **32l** *The fire ceremony,* Codex Borbonicus (BIBLIOTHÈQUE DE L'ASSOCIATION NATIONALE, PARIS) a; **32r** *A scene of anthropophagi,* Codex Magliabechiano (BIBLIOTHÈQUE DU MUSÉE DE L'HOMME, PARIS) a; **34** *Photo portrait of a pygmy* (PRIVATE COLLECTION) a; **35** *Lira* (MUSEO PREISTORICO ED ETNOGRAFICO, ROME) a; **36l** *Paracas Fabric* (PRIVATE COLLECTION) a; **36r** *Andean Band,* Tarabuco festival, Bolivia, (STUART FRANKLIN/MAGNUM/AGENZIA CONTRASTO, ROME) a; **38t** *Tokyo* (BRUNO BARBEY/MAGNUM/AGENZIA CONTRASTO, ROME) a; **38b** *Kabuki Theater* (ARCHIVIO DOGI, FLORENCE) a; **39** *Mask of the noh theater,* Ko-mote, Ashikaga period, 15th century B.C., painted wood (COLLECTION KONGO, TOKYO) a; **40** F. Pourbous, *Ball at the Flanders's court,* (MUSÉE DES BEAUX ARTS, TROYES) d; **41** G. Cariani, *Concert,* painting (PRIVATE COLLECTION, SWITZERLAND) d; **42** Anonymous, *Arrival of Hernán Cortés and of his army in the city of Tlaxcala,* painting, (MUSEO DE LA AMERICA, MADRID) d; **42r** *Mestizo Music* (REDFERNS, LONDON) d; **45** *Taj Mahal* (ARCHIVIO DOGI, FLORENCE) d; **47b** *Farewell, my concubine,* play-bill for the movie by Chen Kaige (I.G.E., ROME) a; **47t** *Genghis Khan leaves to conquer China,* Persian miniature by Shiraz School, 14th century (BRITISH MUSEUM, LONDON) d; **48l** Anonymous, *W. A. Mozart* (DIE GESELLSCHAFT DER MUSIKFREUNDE, VIENNA) d; **48b** *Orchestra Giovanile Italiana* (SCUOLA DI MUSICA DI

FIESOLE/STUDIO ASSOCIATO) a; **48c** *Beethoven's piano* (BEETHOVENHAUS, BONN) a; **49** *Haydn directs a string quartet,* print (MUSEEN DER STADT, VIENNA) a; **50** *Simon Bolivar el Libertador* (RACCOLTA DELLE STAMPE BERTARELLI, MILANO) a; **51t** Anonymous, *Slaves' trade,* engraving (IGDA-RIZZOLI, MILAN) a; **52** *Girl who dances,* Kerry's Puk Fair (H. GRUYAERT/MAGNUM/AGENZIA CONTRASTO, ROME) d; **53b** *Béla Bartok playing the hurdy-gurdy,* c. 1919 (Giancarlo Costa) a; **53t** Marc Chagall, *Gleigenspieler,* 1920, gouache and Kaolin on canvas, 41 × 84 in (213 × 104 cm) (GALLERY TRETJAKOV, MOSQUE) a; **54t** *Charlie Parker* (ARCHIVIO RBA) a; **54b** *Public Enemy* (LA REPUBBLICA, ROME/LONDON FEATURES) a; **55b** *Bessie Smith* (ARCHIVIO NORDISK) d; **56** Paul Colin, *Carlos Gardel,* colored poster (BIBLIOTHÈQUE NATIONALE DE FRANCE, PARIS) d; **57** *Rudolf Valentino dances tango,* photo from the movie "The Four Horsemen of the Apocalypse" by Rex Ingram, 1921 (ARCHIVIO DOGI, FLORENCE) d; **58** *An actor of the Peking Opera* (ARCHIVIO DOGI, FLORENCE) d; **59** *Mao Tse-tung* (XINHUA NEWS AGENCY, PEKING) d; **60** *Elvis* (ARCHIVIO CURCIO, ROME) a; **61** *Alban Berg* (ARCHIVIO DOGI, FLORENCE) d; **62t** *Nusrat Fateh Ali Khan* (LA REPUBBLICA/MAURO VALLINOTTO) a; **62b** *Fela Anikulapo Kuti* (IGDA, MILAN) d.

COVER (clockwise from top left):
1. Costume dell'Opera di Pechino (Archivio DoGi, Florence); **2.** 10; **3.** 11r; **4.** 45; **5.** 26; **6.** 17; **7.** 56; **8.** 49; **9.** 47t; **10.** 51t; **11.** 50; **12.** 57; **13.** 29; **14.** 30; **15.** 55b; **16.** 32r; **17.** 31l; **18.** 23r; **19.** 28t

QUADRANT OF COVER:
Manuela Cappon and Francesco Spadoni.

CONTENTS

THE PROTAGONISTS

This is a geographical and historical atlas of music. It explains how musical languages are born, change, and function in human civilizations in which they are an essential element. Freed from the traditional classifications that separate cultivated from popular music and Western from non-Western music, this is a tale of the routes and interchanges that mark the development of the different musical traditions. Military, political, cultural, and economic events help us to understand this bountiful genesis.

♦ **UNITED STATES**
By examining the most widespread musical genres of this century, we discover that, for the most part, they are born in the United States.

♦ **CENTRAL-SOUTHERN AMERICA**
From pre-Columbian civilizations to the arrival of European colonialists, our journey will cover the drama of the decimation of the natives and of African slavery. It will also reveal how musical traditions flourished from the richness of diverse contributions, the local ones as well as those from a European and African matrix.

♦ **ANCIENT MIDDLE EAST**
A fascinating path leads from the ancient religious music of the Middle East (Egypt, Mesopotamia, and Israel) to the religious music of the European Middle Ages.

♦ EUROPE
In the chapter on European cultivated music, it is fascinating to note the changes in the function of music. From instrument of religious devotion, it transformed into pure entertainment and finally to a true art.

♦ CHINA
From the refined instrumental court music of the millenary Empire to the realistic and revolutionary work of this century's new People's Republic of China.

♦ JAPAN
The Japanese musical tradition undergoes a first period, Aristocratic and Feudal, characterized by court music, and a second one, Bourgeois, linked to theatrical music (*kabuki* and the Puppet Theater).

♦ THE INDIAN SUBCONTINENT
One of the most ancient in the world, the Indian musical tradition has remained the same and yet changed in its often-conflicting relationship with the Moslem culture.

♦ AFRICA
Invaded, colonized, and stripped of its treasures, the African continent has taken its savory revenge. The music of the industrialized Western world is largely indebted to African music.

♦ OCEANIA
Australian aborigines arouse the interest of scholars because they are living examples of a so-called primitive music.

TONES AND COLORS OF AUSTRALIA

In northern Australia, groups of an ancient aboriginal population still live a primitive life. In aboriginal life and cultures, music primarily serves a sacred and magic function. The ancestor gods created the world through chants that guarantee the preservation of life when repeated. Therefore, to ensure their survival, each clan is in charge of performing chants that refer to a single natural phenomenon such as fish, wind, frog, or thunder. This chant becomes the sonorous mark of distinction and identity of each member of the group and allows for a quick recognition during the course of their travels.

♦ AUSTRALIAN ABORIGINES
Very likely, a catastrophic meteorological event affected Australia. The cooling of the climate lowered the sea level, exposing lands that linked New Guinea with Australia by way of the Straits of Torres. Through this natural path almost 15,000 years ago, human scttlements moved from southeastern Asia to Australia. Later on, changes in climate once again separated the island from the continent, preserving it from any contact with outside civilizations. Australian aborigines banded together in small or large groups, traveling to locations where game and natural produce were available. The massive arrival of Europeans in the nineteenth century revolutionized their life-styles. The invaders imposed their laws with violence. Above, an Australian aborigine.

THE PEOPLES OF THE ARNHEM LAND
In the northern tip of Australia, different and perhaps hostile clans meet. The soloist performs few songs to establish an atmosphere of mutual trust and peace.

♦ THE DIJERIDOO
It is the traditional instrument of the aboriginal music, accompanied with rhythm sticks, songs, and dances. Made from a hollow eucalyptus branch, it can produce a legato (melodic) or a syncopated (rhythmic) sound.

♦ **NEW OBJECTS OF CULT**
In the latest aboriginal chants, the most advanced Western technologies appear as cult objects.

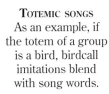

♦ **TOTEM**
It is a natural entity venerated by the clan as its ancestor.

♦ **ETHNOMUSICOLOGY**
This subject was born in the last century out of two needs: to deepen the knowledge of the diverse musical civilizations of the world and to fight the opinion that western classical music is superior to all other musical civilizations. Ethnomusicologists believe that there are neither inferior nor superior musical civilizations. Each one has its own beauty, proper meanings, and values. There is no need to compare them to see which one is the best. Instead, one has to understand the environment, the traditions, and the cultures that have nurtured the music in question. Ethnomusicology also deals with so-called primitive societies in its aim to develop hypotheses on the origin of music. Above, Curt Sachs (1881–1959), the greatest ethnomusicologist of the twentieth century.

TOTEMIC SONGS
As an example, if the totem of a group is a bird, birdcall imitations blend with song words.

♦ **THE SOLOIST**
He tunes songs and leads the dances. He is respected and supported by the community and has the privilege of owning his songs, which cannot be performed without his consent.

♦ **THE CHORUS**
Sometimes, members of the community join the soloist, each modulating his own totemic chant. The result is a magnificent polyvocal mix, where words, strophes, and shouts mix without any preset rule or harmonic plan.

AFRICAN DRUMS

Sub-Saharan Africa is a complex mix of tribes and ethnic groups, each with a specific musical culture. Perhaps their unique common trait is the predominant role of percussion instruments, as the extraordinary variety of drums (slit drums, hourglass drums, and many others) bear witness to. African musicians build rich and complicated interlacing rhythms with their drums. This instrument also has magic and sacred value and it confers power to its owner. For this reason, in eastern Africa, kings own orchestras as well as single drums, which enhance their royal power and strength.

♦ AFRICAN MUSIC AND RHYTHM
To a novice, African music might seem primitive or naïve because of the simplicity of its melodic phrases, reiterated obsessively, and its instrumental accompaniment, often left to drums or rattles. In reality, African music has highly rhythmic, complex compositions. For example, in a western and central African drum composition, the soloist drum starts with a brief and simple rhythmic theme repeated several times. Upon it, other drums intervene, performing different rhythmical themes. A charming effect of polyrhythms is produced, and is reinforced during the course of the performance by frequent variations of rhythms from all the drums involved. Above, a barrel drum from Ghana.

♦ GRIOT
A popular musician in western Africa, he is the depositary of a rich heritage of traditional songs with mythological and epic contents as well as of original compositions on various themes, including politics.

♦ ROYAL DRUMS
They are considered sacred and have magic powers. They receive rich offerings, even from the king.

IN THE SACRED YARD
In Uganda, near the royal village of the Banyankole, there is a sacred area reserved exclusively for the royal drums. No one can enter. Trespassers become untouchable.

♦ THE OFFERINGS
These drums receive daily offerings of milk from sacred cows. Milk is kept a long time in the bowls so that the spirits of the drums can assimilate its essence.

The "wife of the drums" takes care of the royal drums. She covers them for the night and pours the milk offerings. A second woman keeps the fire lit so that the spirits of the drums enjoy the heat.

♦ **AFRICAN ETHNIC GROUPS**
There are three main ethnic groups of sub-Saharan Africa: the Negritic, the Pygmies, and the Koisanide. The first is divided in two sublinguistic groups: the Sudanese and the Bantu. The Sudanese live in northeastern Africa and the Bantu live south of the equator. Materially, they are considered a more advanced civilization. They are familiar with metallurgy and farming. The Koisanide, instead, are nomads and hunt just like the Pygmies. The former inhabit the southern African steppe, while the latter are confined to the equatorial forests, forced to flee by the arrival of stronger Negritic tribes. The Ethiopians constitute a separate ethnic group apart. Above, a Kenyan Masai warrior.

♦ **THE GUARDIAN**
A few guardians protect the royal drums from robbers.

♦ **TALKING DRUMS**
These are African drums, especially slit drums, used to send long-distance messages.

A TEST OF COURAGE

The music of North-American natives shows some characteristics typical of the so-called primitive music such as instrumental poverty, no notation, and most of all, functionality. There is no entertainment music and music is not valued as an art. It may be purposeful, but it is never pleasant or charming for its musical qualities. Music marks every moment of the tribe's life: from the shamans' songs during magic-religious rituals to the community chants before and after battle; and from work songs to courting tunes.

♦ **NORTH-AMERICAN NATIVES**
Before the end of the nineteenth century, Indians lived in hundreds of tribes, each with its own idioms and dialects. Scholars tend to classify Native Americans into roughly ten cultural areas named after the diverse geographical areas they settled in (for example, the Plains Indians). Still it is possible to discover a few traits common to the various cultural areas. For instance, their religion, which considers natural manifestations and, in particular, various elements such as the divine, and the tribal organization in totemic clans. The Europeans arrived during the seventeenth century and then the colonists going west forcefully dislodged them with the aid of federal troops, causing their decimation and transfer into reservations. Above, Native Americans of the Choctaw tribe portrayed in a war scene.

♦ **THE SIOUX**
They were a population divided into many tribes, who traveled the Great Plains between Canada and Nebraska during the seventeenth century.

♦ **A YOUNG WARRIOR**
He is the protagonist of the ceremony. The Sioux believe that warriors have to be kind, brave, and strong-willed. If he succeeds in standing up from dawn to sunset, he gains the respect of the whole community.

THE RITUAL
In the first half of the nineteenth century, several Sioux tribes meet in Dakota. A young warrior has decided to test his indomitable spirit.

♦ JIM MORRISON
The music of the Native Americans influenced both the texts and the vocal style of the lead singer of the Doors, Jim Morrison (at left). He was a rock legend toward the end of the 1960s.

♦ THE MEDICINE MAN
Many cultures of North-American natives believe in the curative power of songs. Their rich spiritual universe relies on a series of relations and interchanges between natural elements and spirits, human and divine, linking wisdom to religion and medicine to magic. The voice not only becomes a human and concrete expression, but also an intangible reality that can talk to the spirits, condition them, and persuade them to reestablish the order that the sickness has altered. The shaman, a man of religion and medicine, in his vocal expressions not only calls for the recovery of the sick man, but also directly intervenes in those material and spiritual realities that have caused the sickness. Above, Howard Terpning, Cheyenne medicine man.

♦ MUSICIANS
They voice ritual songs often characterized by meaningless texts with an extraordinary magic value. They favor a low register and hoarse voices. For the natives, songs can have two origins: musical skill and visions, the latter bestowing the songs upon them.

♦ INSTRUMENTS
Instrumental accompaniment is limited to a few percussion instruments such as drums, rattles, and sticks. Courting tunes, performed by flutes, are the only exception.

♦ BLACK ELK
He was one of the most highly respected shamans of the Sioux. With the help of a scholar of comparative religious studies, he wrote a book in which he explained the philosophical, religious, and spiritual universe of the Sioux.

WAVING RHYTHM

For a long time, the peoples of the oceanic archipelagos managed to repel all foreign invasions, preserving their original traditions and lifestyles thanks to their combative character and their seductive, but perilous environment. The ocean is the center of their lives, the source of their economy, culture, and music. The ocean is the dominant theme of their songs and dances; from it, the skillful Polynesian artisans extract the material to make their musical instruments.

OCEAN BAIT
In a beach of the Marchesi Islands, in French Polynesia, the catch of some sharks will provide the group with the basic material for their drums.

♦ HAKA SONGS AND DANCES
In the repertoire of the Maori of New Zealand, there are war songs and dances spiked with insults and menaces toward the enemy.

♦ SHELLS
Polynesians make trumpets from shells. They also use shell fragments to create *sistrums,* used as rattles to lure sharks into traps.

♦ LOCAL CANOES
To catch sharks, islanders employ outrigger canoes, typical oceanic deep-sea dugouts.

♦ THE SHARK
Once captured, the shark is quartered for its skin, which is needed for drumheads.

Around 2000 B.C., the first groups populating Melanesia and Micronesia left Indonesia. Between 1000 and 500 B.C., the same groups reached the faraway islands of Polynesia. They moved not only in response to their spirit of adventure, but also in response to need. Whenever an island lacked enough resources for all the members of the group, the youngest usually left in search of uninhabited, but prosperous, islands. They set off in their deep-sea outriggers with the help of ingenious nautical maps made of rushes (showing winds and currents), interwoven with shells (representing islands). Above, a girl from a Polynesian atoll.

♦ DRUMS
Generally, Polynesian drums are cylindrical, have a narrow central diameter, and are open at the bottom.

THE EXCAVATIONS OF UR

Expert in geometry, astronomy, and architecture, the ancient Mesopotamian civilization (a term that encompasses almost 2500 years of history and events affecting different populations) cultivated music. In the Mesopotamian temples, in particular, the presence of instrumentalists and choristers was required for the liturgy. Soloists chanted accompanied by lyres, harps, and percussion instruments. Choirs alternated with the soloist in tuning prayers into a form that is surprisingly similar to the form adopted by the Christian church many centuries later. Deprived of natural frontiers, the Mesopotamian region promoted exchanges among various Middle Eastern civilizations, which facilitated the journey of its musical instruments across Egypt and other lands.

♦ **THE HISTORY OF MESOPOTAMIA**
In 3000 B.C., the Sumerians settled in the lower area of Mesopotamia, starting a civilization whose main traits would be assimilated even by its later invaders: the Babylonians. The Sumerians were highly knowledgeable in the fields of astronomy and science and were able to work metals. They built towns, roads, and canals. They organized themselves into a state ruled by a king-priest under whom merchants, craftsmen, and slaves were deployed within a hierarchy. Around 1700 B.C., the Semitic Babylonians replaced the Sumerians. Their king, Hammurabi, founded an empire that collapsed in the eleventh century when confronted by the Assyrians, another Semitic population, much more aggressive than their precedessors. Above, a board game found at Ur, with shell and stone tokens.

♦ **THE HARP**
Made of wood, it shone with lapis lazulis and a golden bullhead bulging out of the soundbox. Over it rests the skeleton of a man who died suddenly while playing.

♦ **A TROUBLING DISCOVERY**
During one excavating campaign (1922–1934), near the temple of the Sumerian town of Ur, several royal tombs dating from around 2500 B.C. were discovered. Soon thereafter, the excavation team discovered an astounding and horrific scene.

♦ **LEONARD WOOLEY**
(1880–1960) British archaeologist acclaimed for the discovery of the necropolis of Ur. He narrated the details of his findings in breathtaking books of great scientific value.

14

♦ THE ZIGGURAT
It is a step pyramid with a temple at its summit. It was the apogee around which the economic, social, and religious life of ancient Mesopotamia revolved.

♦ HYPOTHESES
The discovery of the lonely skeleton of a princess, in another part of the necropolis, solved the mystery. Apparently, the court of the deceased princess decided to follow her in the afterlife. Accompanied by the customary tunes and chants of the Sumerian funerals, the faithful courtiers had poisoned themselves.

♦ THE GOBLETS
Goblets lay beside the skeletons. Soon, the archaeologists suspected that the goblets might have contained poison, voluntarily drunk by the women and by the harpist.

♦ THE SKELETONS
Arranged along two rows, they wore luxurious head coverings and pearl necklaces.

EGYPTIAN HARMONIES

Two universes coexist in the music of ancient Egypt. The first, mysterious and archaic, is a reminder that the divine reveals itself in sound and the second, modern and manifest, empowers music with the task of bringing joy to its listeners. Therefore, both religious and entertainment music existed in ancient Egypt. Both types of music, although modified during the course of the centuries, present an abundance of harps, lyres, and lutes, signs that ancient Egyptians preferred the melodic rather than the rhythmical aspects of music.

♦ **THE HISTORY OF ANCIENT EGYPT**
Usually, the history of ancient Egypt is divided into three periods: the Old Kingdom, the Middle Kingdom, and the New Kingdom. The Old Kingdom dates back to circa 2700 B.C., after the unification of the country under the rule of its first pharaoh, King Menes. The Old Kingdom marks the beginning of one of the most advanced civilizations of the epoch, characterized by a variety of professions, many scientific discoveries, and monumental constructions such as the pyramids, which were the pharaohs' funerary tombs. During the Middle Kingdom, Thebes became the new capital. The New Kingdom was the period of maximum splendor. A period of decadence followed, culminating with the foreign ruling of the Macedonian king, Alexander the Great (332 B.C.). Above, a bust of Queen Nefertiti.

♦ **THE PHARAOH AMENHOTEP IV**
He founded the city of Tell el Amarna and promoted a religious and artistic reform that introduced the new cult of the solar disk and greater realism in the figurative representation of the royal highnesses.

A NEW RELIGION
Toward the first half of the fourteenth century B.C., in the temple of Tell el Amarna dedicated to Aten (the sun god), Amenhotep IV, accompanied by his wife, Nefertiti, and their daughters, made offerings to Aten, a new deity.

♦ **AN ANCIENT MAESTRO**
He directed the instrumental and choral ensemble that accompanied the ritual. To show the flow of the melody, he used specific hand gestures, a technique known as chironomy.

♦ INSTRUMENTS
During the New Kingdom, religious music became livelier, more animated, and richer in instruments. Rituals were no longer exclusively accompanied by flutes, oboes, and bow harps.

♦ FEMALE MUSICIANS
During the New Kingdom, noble priestesses worked in the temple. They were called "the wives of the god." During the course of the rituals, they also acted as musicians, playing tambourines and often sistrums, sacred instruments preferred by the princesses.

♦ THE BOW HARP
It is the symbol of ancient Egyptian music. During the New Kingdom, three kinds of bow harps existed. The angle harp, the bow-shaped harp, and the shoulder harp. Later, the number of strings and dimensions of the angle harp increased.

♦ MUSIC IN THE FIELDS
Figurative reproductions of musicians accompanying the work in the fields abounded. Sometimes, music had a religious function, but at other times, it set the rhythm of the work itself.

THE MUSIC OF THE BIBLE

The Bible is the sacred revered text of Jews and Christians and a bountiful compendium of news on practical issues as well as on the musical life of ancient Middle Eastern populations. For the nomadic Jewish tribes, music celebrated the only God, Yahweh, and was the product of collective improvisation. With the birth of the Kingdom of Israel (circa 1000 B.C.) and the construction of the Temple of Jerusalem, liturgical celebrations were enhanced by professional singers and musicians. However, it was in the synagogues built after the destruction of the first temple (587 B.C.) that the forms of sung liturgies took shape. These partially transferred to the eastern Christians and, later on, to the western Christians, which echoed in churches like mysterious remembrances of an archaic Middle East.

♦ THE JEWISH PEOPLE
Once nomadic shepherds of monotheist religion, arriving in Palestine around 1300 B.C., the Jewish people gradually became farmers. They also changed their political system from patriarchal to monarchic. Their first king was Saul (circa 1000 B.C.), who was succeeded by David and then Solomon, who moved the capital to Jerusalem, and built a temple there. When he died, the nation split into the Kingdoms of Israel and Judah. The Babylonians wrecked the temple and deported the Jews to Babylonia (587 B.C.). With the victory of the Persian king Cyrus over the Babylonians, the Jews returned to Palestine and rebuilt the temple. In 63 B.C., Palestine became a Roman province. A Jewish revolt was repressed in 70 A.D. with the destruction of the second temple. The Diaspora of the Jews in the world thus began. Above, Jewish worshippers at the Wailing Wall in Jerusalem.

THE EXILE
Circa 587 B.C., the Jews were deported to Babylonia from the flock of King Nebuchadnezzar. Distant from Palestine and enslaved in a foreign kingdom, the Jews hang the kinnor from the willow tree, which seemed joyful considering the state of their imprisonment.

♦ TORAH
After saving them from the destruction of a temple, a priest holds the rolls of the Jewish sacred text, the Torah, including the first five books of the Old Testament.

♦ NEVEL
A Jewish harp handled by a Levite. The Jews believed that only particular social groups could play some types of instruments. Priests, for instance, had the privilege of playing trumpets and animal horns, while popular classes practiced on flutes, cymbals, and drums. The Levites played string instruments.

♦ BABYLONIA
The Jewish
people remained
in Babylonia
until the Persian
King, Cyrus the
Great, permitted
them to return to
Palestine in 538
B.C., after having
defeated the
Babylonians.

♦ FROM THE
TEMPLE TO THE
SYNAGOGUE
A chorus of
20,000 people,
accompanied by
kinnors, harps,
and cymbals, sing
hymns to Yahweh.
This image dates
back to the
kingdoms of King
David and his son,
Solomon
(1004–926 B.C.).
Under their
reigns, music
shifted hands. It
was no longer
freely played by
ordinary people,
but only by a
professional class
of musicians,
chosen from the
Levite tribe. They
were entitled to
perform during
religious
ceremonies,
always close to
the rich Egyptian
liturgies. The
destruction of the
temple brought
about the rise of
new religious
sites, synagogues,
which were more
modest and where
music relied only
upon vocal
singing. The sung
liturgy was
divided into
psalmody, the
tuning of psalms
on a single
iterated note, and
cantillations, a
way of reading the
Bible, halfway
between reciting
and singing.
Above, the inside
of a synagogue.

♦ THE LEVITES
They belonged
to a Jewish tribe
and mainly took
care of religion-
related matters,
including musical
ones. They
received their
musical training
at the school
annexed to the
temple.

♦ KINNOR (THE LYRE)
Jewish people
played the kinnor,
the ancient Jewish
lyre. It was King
David's favorite
instrument and he
played it to accom-
pany the psalms
he composed.

AULOS AND KITHARA

In ancient Greece, music, poetry, and theater blended together. Poetic strophes were always recited with a music background and musical pieces never stood out without poetic lines. Poets were also musicians and lyrical genres were also musical genres. This interaction of music and poetry influenced the characters of the two arts. Thus, music was mostly vocal, respectful of words that always had to be understood (the rigid correspondence between syllables and notes served this purpose). Only at the onset of the fifth century B.C. did this separate, and forms of solely instrumental music evolved amidst the objections of traditionalists.

♦ THE HISTORY OF GREECE
Greek civilization originated from the migrations of an Indo-European population, the Achaens, who assimilated the then flourishing Cretan civilization. At the beginning of the eighth century B.C., after the Dark Ages that followed the Doric domination, a revival ran through the country. It reached its climax during the fifth century with an intense economic development, a vivacious political season, and vivid intellectual ferment. It was the time when, in politics, democratic principles were established (especially in Athens) and philosophy and classical art came to light. Divided into many *poleis,* independent city-state nuclei, the Greeks defended their freedom against the expansionist goals of Persians and Athenians. In the end, however, they succumbed to the fury of King Philip of Macedonia, who, in 338 B.C., unified Greece under his rule. Above, the Parthenon.

A MUSICAL INTERMEZZO
In Delphi, at the end of the Pythian competitions dedicated to Apollo, the winners of the musical competitions for the kithara (lyre) and aulos (oboe), assemble at a noble's villa. They improvise a dance performance of the myth of Apollo, who defeated Marsyas in a musical challenge.

♦ THE SINGER
To play the aulos (oboe) demanded skill. However, the traditional supremacy attributed by Greek music to the word tinged the singer with more respect than the musician.

♦ AULOS
It is an oboe with a penetrating and strident sound. It accompanies the rites in honor of Dionysus. Greek tradition sees it as the symbol of wild Eastern impulsiveness.

♦ MARSYAS
He was a native of Asia Minor. It is claimed that he invented the aulos. He challenged Apollo, the lyre player, in a musical competition, which he lost.

♦ ODYSSEY
The music of both *The Iliad* and *The Odyssey* is presented here, which shows a singer accompanied by the kitharas. It will be a bard, narrating the events of the Trojan War, who brings Odysseus to tears and escapes his vengeful strike against suitors.

♦ MUSIC AND EDUCATION
The Greeks believed that music had the power of stirring souls and wills. It educated, but also corrupted, brought joy or folly. Therefore, music was both a resource and a danger. Or so Plato thought. His position facing the musical revolution that started in the fifth century and lasting until the fourth, was that of a critic. He criticized music's exaggerated noisy character, the search for easy musical effects, and the desire of bringing only pleasure to listeners. Instead, Plato deemed that music had to aim at moral and righteous objectives. It had to embody musical forms that operated positively over the individual by injecting more self-confidence and respect for the universal laws that govern the world. Above, Raphael, *The School of Athens*, 1509–1510, Rome, Vatican Palace, detail of Plato's portrait.

♦ APOLLO
The dancer interprets the role of Apollo, son of Zeus, god of the arts and inventor of the lyre. The Greeks saw in his mythical victory over Marsyas, the supremacy of moderation, harmony, and equilibrium (typical values of the classical Greek civilization) over the sensuality and disorder of the East.

♦ KITHARA
It is a seven-stringed lyre originally made of hemp. It accompanies poetry. Played especially by professionals during concerts and Panhellenic games, it never overtakes singing or voices.

CHINESE STORIES AND LEGENDS

According to the ancient Chinese tradition, sound is part of the universe and has a central role in its eternal functioning. A good musical performance ensures the virtuous order of the cosmos, while mistakes may cause disorder and natural calamities. Therefore, music is a state affair, deserving the creation of an Imperial Music Bureau. The power of music is the power of sound, which is not a simple note fleeing from a musical instrument, but a magic force that escapes from material friction or a strike by the performer. Hence, the singular Chinese classification of instruments is based on their material rather than on the modality of sounds they produce.

♦ THE HISTORY OF ANCIENT CHINA
Already between the third and the second millennium B.C., the villages around the Yellow River organized themselves into a state, governed at the beginning of the sixteenth century B.C. by the Shang dynasty. In 1122 B.C., the Chou dynasty replaced it. Between 475 and 221 B.C., the weakness of the ruling dynasty contributed to the creation of independent principalities. One of their kings conquered all the Chinese territories, electing himself the first emperor under the name of Shi Huangdi. The Han dynasty (206 B.C.–220 A.D.) followed. It was a period of orderly bureaucratic efficiency. Four hundred years of disorder went by, causing the division of the empire into three kingdoms. The Sui dynasty (581–618) unified China. It was, however, the T'ang dynasty (618–907) that brought new prosperity, greater prestige for the army, and a considerable flourishing of the arts. Above, the Great Wall.

♦ COURT MUSICIANS
Some court musicians furtively bury venerable ancient carillon bells to spare them from the devastating fury of the soldiers.

♦ CARILLON BELLS
For the Chinese, a sound with magic power is evoked by the substance; hence, the sacredness of those instruments that produce the sound by vibration of their own materials. Carillon bells are among them. They are more numerous than the string instruments and carry a melodic function.

TRADITION GOES UP IN SMOKE
In 213 B.C., in Ch'ang-an, the Emperor Shi Huangdi burned all the history, philosophy, and music books to forbid anyone to consider tradition or to criticize his drastic reform of the Chinese state.

♦ CONFUCIUS
He was a philosopher who lived between the sixth and the fifth century B.C. He developed a moral and political doctrine that forced princes to govern through music and rituals. He believed that music could soothe the soul with peaceful feelings, promoting education. At left, an image of Confucius.

♦ COURT MUSIC
The power of music convinced Chinese emperors to exert a careful surveillance over it. The effort to classify and standardize music was constant. For this reason, the *Book of Music,* a chapter included in the *Book of Rites* (second century B.C.) was a court classic. During the Han period, a music bureau opened up to collect the national musical repertoire and to verify that court music was correctly executed. During the T'ang period, court music knew its golden days, as reported in an official document known as *The Imperial Lists of Ten Kinds of Music.* From that moment on, court music included, in addition to the national repertoire, music and dances of Korea, India, and Central Asia. Above, a terracotta sculpture from the T'ang period.

♦ SHI HUANGDI
In 221, he became the first Emperor of China. He tried to unify this immense land under his authority. He challenged the feudal lords and unified currency, weights, and measurements.

HINDU MUSIC

In the sacred Hindu texts and in the ancient philosophical Indian treatises, music is a supernatural force able to affect man's destiny and to influence the gods. Thanks to its power, music pervades every aspect of Indian religious life. It is present during sacrificial rites, where the correct intonation of formulas guarantees the success of the rite, as well as amidst individual prayers, marked by the recitation of sonorous syllables. It accompanies the performance of epic-religious poems (the *Ramayana* and the *Mahabharata*) and the tuning of sacred texts.

♦ THE HISTORY OF INDIA
Around 1500 B.C., the Indo-European Aryans invaded India. They imposed their own religion based on the Vedas (sacred texts). The fulcrum of ancient Indian society is the rigid division into castes, that is to say, into social classes that have no contact with one another. Subject to the Persian and Macedonian dominations, India was unified by King Asoka during the third century B.C. He converted to Buddhism, the new religion that soon spread across the country. Other invasions followed. First, the Kusanas, originating in central Asia, crossed the northern border and then, between 335 and 376, the Kingdom of the Gupta dynasty ruled. During the Gupta period, trade developed and poetry flourished. At the beginning of the eighth century, after the Hun domination, Arabs occupied northern India for the first time. Above, a Hindu temple.

♦ THE TABLA
The tabla plays an important role in the music of accompaniment of Ramlila. It is especially common in northern India.

♦ AUDIENCES
They follow the events on the stage with a dazzling emotional commitment. They venerate the actors, believing that they are the true incarnations of their worshipped deities.

♦ THE SITAR
It is of Moslem origin, but it is surely one of the most common instruments of northern India. Most likely, it is derived from the Persian lute setar.

♦ THE KATAKALI DANCE-DRAMA
It is a genre born in southern India around 1700. It is a refined mix of dance, music, and singing with a complicated, but fascinating language of gestures and movements. It is one of the main subjects of Rama's epic poem.

RAMLILA

In a street of Benares (Varanasi), a scene from *Ramlila* is playing, a musical and theatrical representation of the *Ramayana,* the Hindu sacred epic poem. It requires frequent changes of scene around town. It even includes the crossing of the Ganges.

✦ THE VEDAS
Perhaps the oldest Indian cultivated music genre is the intonation of the Vedas, the sacred texts of the religion introduced by the Aryans.

✦ MUSIC AND CASTES
In India, music is part of philosophy and religion. This influences not only musical theory, but also musical genres and the manner of performing music. For instance, the preference accorded to the vocal genre had a philosophical-religious basis (the voice was conceived as pure sound), not a musical one (a penchant for vocal timbres). So, Indian musicians' dislikes for any fusion of voices or melodies (i.e. polyphony) originated from the religious compliance with the principle of rigid segmentation of society into castes. Indians believed that this division corresponded to a universal order that could never be questioned by any social or musical form of fusion. Above, a Hindu.

✦ THE GENERAL OF THE MONKEY BAND
He helps Rama free his wife Sita, kidnapped by Ravan, the evil king.

✦ RAMA
According to Hindu mythology, it is the seventh avatar of the god Vishnu, and the brave and right-eous hero of the *Ramayana,* the ancient epic poem in Sanskrit, a reference text on Indian culture.

IMPERIAL CONCERTS

Court orchestra music (*gagaku*) was introduced in Japan during the seventh century A.D. Inspired by the Chinese, it is among the most ancient musical traditions of the world. It was only for aristocrats, who in a fragile alliance with the emperor, ruled the state. It entertained the court, boosted the power of the emperor, and accompanied important religious ceremonies. Performed by rich orchestral ensembles, playing at first only foreign music (mostly Chinese), *gagaku* demonstrated over time the valuable gift of the Japanese culture to rework foreign elements along the lines of their national taste.

♦ THE HISTORY OF JAPAN
The rise of Japan as a united state goes back to a late epoch of the country's history. In 700 A.D., the emperor, inspired by the Chinese model, was capable of ruling over a very powerful and autonomous aristocracy. He became the undisputed political and religious head of the nation with the support of the nobles, who held essential positions in the management and politics of the country. Around 1000 A.D., the court aristocracy replaced the emperor. Because it ruled from the capital, its power was weak in the provinces, where local grandees relinquished neither independence nor prestige. Above, Japanese art of the Nara period.

♦ DANCES
Court dances accompanied by the orchestra music *gagaku* are a precious and difficult art. They demand refined skills and great precision. They aim at pleasing audiences, not personal whims.

♦ **MUSICIANS**
They were professionals and usually belonged to the local aristocracy.

Later, court nobles turned from spectators into amateur *gagaku* performers.

♦ **SHINTO MUSIC**
Among the various forms of *gagaku,* there is the ritual music for Shinto ceremonies. Today, Shintoism is still the most popular religion in Japan, although it has lost its character as a national religion. In the court temple and in front of the emperor, performers played music that, contrary to *kangen* and *bugaku,* originated from the inception of archaic Japanese music rather than from acculturation of foreign models. The vocal style and the instruments that accompany Shinto songs display an original character. The instrumental composition of the orchestra is different from the *kangen*. Three types of instruments form it: a flute and two zithers. In Shinto rites, dances of religious or mythic arguments are often present. Generally, four or six dancers interpret it. Above, a bronze sculpture.

♦ **THE ORCHESTRA**
It executes pieces of the *gagaku* repertoire. During the ninth century, this was divided into music of the left side (Chinese and Indian repertoires) and music of the right side (Korean and Manchu repertoires).

FROM BAGHDAD TO CORDOBA

When Arab knights, inflamed by their new faith in Allah and the lust for money, started their round of conquests (at the beginning of the seventh century B.C.), a musical tradition was already in place in the Arabian peninsula. Prostitute singers (*qainat*) kept it alive. They tuned various songs into a florid vocal style either in the markets of Mecca or in pleasure houses. It was, however, during the rise of the huge empire, that traditional Arab music civilization established itself harmoniously with the Byzantine, Syrian, and especially Persian musical civilizations. The *ud* (lute), a symbol of Arab music, was Persian, as were some of the most remarkable musicians, who were admired and hosted in the refined courts of emirs and caliphs.

♦ THE ARABS
Shepherds, farmers, and along the coast, even merchants, the inhabitants of the Arabian peninsula achieved religious and political union thanks to the words and actions of the prophet Mohammed (570–632 A.D.). The new state was governed by a caliph, a religious and political figure. This position soon fell (661 A.D.) into the hands of the dynasty of the Ommanyadi. Swiftly, the Arabs overpowered Persia, Palestine, Egypt, North Africa, and Spain. This colossal empire was shaken by conflicts between Arab and non-Arab populations and between noble families. In the end, the Abbassidi family overpowered everyone else. In 762, they moved the capital to Baghdad and thus the epoch of greatest splendor for the empire began. Local governors (*emirs*), however, undermined it. They formed independent caliphates that broke the unity of the empire. Above, Arab warriors.

♦ ISLAM
It is a monotheist religion founded by Mohammed in the seventh century A.D. The *Koran,* the Moslem sacred text, lays out its precepts. In the Koran, music was considered a forbidden pleasure. Left, Moslems in pilgrimage to Mecca.

THE FUGUE
In 822, the famous lute player and singer, Zyriab, landed in Cordoba after fleeing the court of Baghdad. There, the jealousy of his maestro had made his life miserable.

♦ **CORDOBA**
It was the capital of the new emirate established in Spain in 756 A.D. It was a lively cultural and artistic town. In the thirteenth century, the Arab philosophy passed to France via Cordoba and medieval Europe opened its doors to the *ud*.

♦ **DIFFERENT STYLES**
When the capital of the empire moved to Baghdad, Arab music elaborated the ancient pre-Islamic tradition, giving life to the eastern style. Vocal and instrumental, it relied on the improvisation of the soloist, accompanied by small orchestras. Lute, flute, zither, and frame drums composed them. The luxurious performances with more than two hundred instrumentalists in the palace of Baghdad, during the reign of the caliph Al-Rashid (around 800 A.D.), did not last. Independent emirates, like that of Cordoba, in Spain, produced the western style. Compared to the eastern style, it had less freedom from the melodic and rhythmic schemes of the tradition. The composition of the orchestras was also different. Above, inside an Andalusian mosque.

♦ **ZYRIAB**
He was born in Baghdad. The musician Al-Mausili, who immediately recognized his talent, introduced him to the court of the caliph. Composer and theoretician, he is considered the father of western-style Arab music.

♦ **UD**
It is a short-necked lute, of Persian origin. Zyriab increased the number of its strings from four to five. He also introduced the use of a plectrum made of an eagle's feather, replacing the traditional wooden one. Moreover, he color-coded the strings, matching them with different moods, according to the western-style habit of linking music with philosophy or psychology.

THE SCHOLA CANTORUM

The music of medieval Europe was the music of the Roman Catholic church, whose values at the end of the western Roman empire gave life to a new civilization. Performed mostly in monasteries and churches, the sole purpose of music was to glorify God. Bound to Greek musical theory, in its practical execution it echoed the music employed in the Jewish liturgy for its tuned recitation of the Bible and the exclusion of instrumental music. At last, the need to unify liturgical chants all over Europe animated the first examples of musical notation. Examples are the *neum,* a graphic sign that indicated the movement of the melody and the *tetragram* (a set of four musical lines), with which it became easier to establish the pitch of the sound.

♦ **GREGORIAN CHANTS**
Because of the enormous distances, poor communication among Christian communities and, above all, the sheer freedom enjoyed by local churches, many liturgies and related chants once existed in Europe. To face such a variety, the church opted for a Roman rite (Latin), starting during the sixth century to execute a repertoire of what are called Gregorian chants. Gregorian chants have a monophonic texture. They exhibit one voice only (they will be adopted for polyphonic experiments at a later epoch), and have no instrumental accompaniment because instruments were too bound to pagan rites. They are divided into antiphonic chants (performed by two alternating choruses) and responsorial chants (performed in alternation between soloist and chorus). Above, the score of a Gregorian chant.

A DAY AT CLUNY
Early in 1100 A.D., the chorus of the Schola Cantorum rehearsed, while in the scriptorium, amanuenses transcribed Gregorian melodies on precious books.

♦ **THE SCHOLA CANTORUM**
From spontaneous collective participation, it shifted to a body of professional cantors (Schola Cantorum) charged with performing Gregorian chants during the liturgy.

♦ THE TROUBADOURS
Usually nobles joined the official music, which was composed by and for the church. They tuned songs in the *langue d'oc* (dialect of southern France), mostly dealing with matters of love. At left, German troubadours at court.

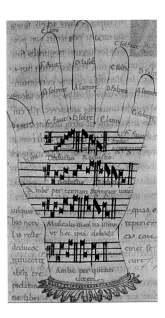

♦ MUSICAL DIDACTIC
During the Middle Ages, numerous pages of didactic were written. Among the most popular, the *Micrologus* by the Benedictine monk Guido D'Arezzo, a work aimed at training the cantors of Episcopal and monastic schools. At left, the "Guidonian Hand" with the notes Do, Re, Mi, Fa, Sol, La, and Ti.

♦ THE EARLIEST FORMS OF POLYPHONY
Already during the ninth century in France, polyphony (many-voiced singing) was being tentatively shaped.
During the performance of a Gregorian chant, for instance, one of the two voices (tenor) conducted the singing while the other separated from the tenor and executed the same chant at a higher pitch. At first, for every note tuned by the tenor, a note of the second voice had to match. Hence, the term counter-point (point— or better note— against point) was coined. Then, skillful French theoreticians and composers elaborated polyphony. The contrary move-ment (*descant*) of the two voices replaced their parallel movement. The number of voices increased and polyphonic solutions were assembled, found-ed on the rhythmic contrast of the two voices (no more note against note). Above, inside a Gothic cathedral.

♦ THE ABBEY OF CLUNY
Founded in 910, it rose as a Benedictine abbey. Later, it hosted the autonomous Cluniac congregation, at the base of an important spiritual reform of the church. After the French revolution (1790), it was suppressed.

♦ THE SCRIPTORIUM
A room annexed to the library, where amanuenses patiently copied texts. Few Cluny manuscripts with *neumatic* notation survived.

SACRED DANCES

The Aztecs, who at the end of 1400 A.D., before the arrival of the Europeans, spread their influence across a wide area corresponding to modern-day Central America, considered music a community activity. There were numerous "Houses of Singing" (*Cuicalli*). These were rooms annexed to temples, reserved for anyone older than twelve wishing to sing and play. Professionalism did not lack. In fact, professional musicians and singers enjoyed public respect and esteem, probably because of the role they played in religious ceremonies. Rich in percussion, rattles, and wind instruments, the Aztecs did not have string instruments.

♦ HUMAN SACRIFICES
The religion and rituality of the Aztec people included human sacrifices, often preceded by theatrical shows accompanied by music. The victim used to play the role of the god, the main part.

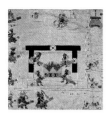

♦ THE AZTECS
Originally, the Aztecs lived in the south of what is now the United States. They split into warlike tribes and hunted. They moved to the plains of Mexico when they heard of the military difficulties of the Toltecs, the dominant tribe in the region at the time (twelfth century A.D.). Soon, they absorbed the technological discoveries of the Toltec people, especially the art of pottery. They also adopted their religion and political organization. From a tribal egalitarian society, they shifted to a hierarchical society ruled by an emperor (the political leader). They quit being nomadic hunters and became farmers. Their capital, Tenochtitlán, famous for its impressive temples, became at the end of 1400 A.D. the most important political-military center of the region. Above, the "Ceremony of the Fire" in an Aztec representation.

♦ DRUMS
The slit drum, *teponaztli,* and the footed drum, *thalpanhuéhuetl,* enlivened dances. Considered sacred instruments, they were lifted to avoid contamination.

♦ DANCES
The Aztecs were excellent dancers, admired for the precision and beauty of their movements. They believed that poetry, music, and dance were connected. For this reason, the recitation of poems enlightened dances.

THE LONG DANCE OF THE AZTECS
In the ceremonial square of
Tenochtitlán, the Aztec capital,
ritual dances dedicated to the
goddesses of earth took place.
Dances continued for hours,
with choreography involving
only hand and arm movements.

✦ **DANCE
MISFORTUNES**
For the Aztecs,
to make dance
mistakes meant
to sin. Wrong

dance steps
brought punish-
ment and even
a summary
execution.

✦ **THE EMPEROR**
Even the emperor
joined the dances,
hoping to win the
favor of the gods.

THE MASTERS OF POLYPHONY

Whoever thinks that nontechnological and nonscientific societies share an equally poor spiritual destiny is wrong. The complex polyphonic chants of the Pygmies prove it. In the pluvial forests of Central Africa, the primitive communities of Pygmies generate collective songs where groups or, more rarely, soloists tune identical melodic lines. They join in at different times, overlapping along a scheme that recalls a typical canon of European counterpoint. Even the vocal style is complex, close to European yodeling, with the quick movement from a chest voice (low register) to a falsetto (high register).

♦ THE PYGMIES
The first record of the Pygmies dates back to the epoch of the ancient Egyptian civilization. Pharaohs organized hunting games to capture these small men, approximately 4 to 5 feet (1.3–1.5 m) tall. Pygmies were famous for their musical skills. This is not surprising. Music always played a fundamental role in their community. At a very early age, mothers initiated their children to music. Pygmies hunted with a simple bow or metal-pointed spears. Negritic populations, with whom they had established good neighborhood relationships, had introduced them to pointed spears. The Pygmies believe in a supreme being as well as in good and evil spirits, the latter being responsible for sickness. Above, a girl in a photo dating from the end of the nineteenth century.

A FAN
In his office, Louis Sarno, an American ethnomusicologist, listens to recordings of Pygmy songs. He recorded them during his sojourn with the Ba-Benjeli Pygmies.

♦ POLYPHONY
Sarno believes that the polyphony of Pygmy chants, where every melodic line is equally important, expresses the egalitarian character of their society.

♦ DRUMS
Sometimes small drums accompany Pygmy songs and dances during performances for outsiders.

♦ THE VILLAGE
Louis Sarno is with his newly found friends in a Negritic village. He discovered that Pygmies, in front of outsiders, perform chants and music different from the ones they reserve for the forest, their magic place.

♦ AFRICA AND MELODY
Although rhythm is the dominant characteristic of African music, the melodic dimension is not absent completely. Polyphonic chants of Pygmies and southern African groups like Zulu and Xhoto-Xhoto, as well as the most popular and typical call and response and antiphonal forms prove this. In the first case, a soloist voices the chant and the chorus answers with a brief melodic formula. In the second case, two choruses alternate. Additionally, there are African regions where the melodic character becomes stronger with the presence of the Islamic religion. In the Sudan, for instance, the arrival of Moslem people spread the ancient Arab musical tradition, string instruments, and the peculiarly florid Arab vocal style. Above, a large wooden lyre.

♦ LOUIS SARNO
He is an ethno-musicologist, a native of New Jersey. One evening, in a European capital, he listened by chance to a Pygmy song on the radio. He decided at once to study that original musical tradition.

THE EMPEROR'S ARMY

Even today, the notes of quena (flute) orchestras flow across the Andean plateaus. They echo the ancient musical tradition of the Incas, characterized by many different flutes, whistles, and trumpets, often superbly built and refinished by skillful ceramists. For the Incas, music accompanied religious ceremonies and played an important element in their military life. Trumpets announced the arrival of the emperor's armies, drums beat to the troops marching, musical shouts animated the battle, and war songs celebrated victories and signals triumphed in the capital.

♦ THE CIVILIZATION OF THE INCAS
The empire of the Incas established itself relatively late (1438) and, lasted only one century (1438–1531). Nonetheless, during its hegemonic campaigns, it absorbed local populations, and the characteristics of the most ancient Andean civilizations (the Mochica and the Chimu) filtered to the top. The Inca Empire distinguished itself by its centralized hierarchical state organization. At the head of their political establishment was the king, a god on earth, whose orders were promptly obeyed everywhere in the empire thanks to a disciplined and efficient administration. The Incas knew about metallurgy and pottery. They fertilized the land and practiced an advanced technological surgical technique using anesthesia, most likely with coca leaves. Above, a fabric that portrays the pattern of the trophy-head.

♦ QUENA ORCHESTRAS
It was a typical orchestral band of the Andes. Originally, every Andean community had a quena orchestra, each with its own peculiar traits (diverse intonation and different number of quenas). These distinctive characteristics helped people to immediately recognize where they came from.

♦ PRISONERS
The Incas were benevolent toward war prisoners. They carried them to the capital to show them off, but in the end, they sent them home.

♦ INCA SOLDIERS
Equipped with spears and axes, they endured a tough discipline.

After winning a battle, the Inca army returns to the capital loaded with riches and prisoners.

♦ TRUMPETS
The Incas used terracotta hooked trumpets. Messengers played them mainly to signal the presence of marching armies.

♦ DRUMS
Often, the skin of defeated prisoners covered the drumheads.

OSAKA'S PUPPETS

In the still agricultural and feudal Japan of the thirteenth and fourteenth centuries, two new musical genres developed: the epic narration accompanied by the *biwa* (lute) and the music for the Noh theater. The latter was an art form where singing, recitation, music, and dance merged. Besides the Noh, which was performed only for aristocrats, two new and more popular theaters evolved in the changed scene of seventeenth-century Japan: kabuki and puppet theater. Preferred by Osaka's rich merchants and small artisans at the end of the seventeenth century, puppet theater added even more prestige to the popular genre of the *shamisen* (lute) music.

♦ THE HISTORY OF JAPAN
In 1185, the creation of the shogunate, which sanctioned the military leadership of great noble families over the emperor, did not solve the central government's weakness. It stopped neither the fighting among the grand lords nor the threat of an internal division. The rise of a mercantile class, due to internal trade development and exchanges with China, altered the ancient social feudal-aristocratic structure. In the sixteenth century, after the arrival of the first Europeans, the Japanese leadership decided to close frontiers (1639). During the nineteenth century, Japan received pressures to reopen to American ships. Following this, Mutsuhito reestablished the authority of the emperor (the Meiji period). He promoted a bold program of economic reforms, which oriented Japan toward today's modernization. Above, a view of Tokyo.

♦ KABUKI
It is a lively synthesis of chants, dialogues, danced pantomimes, and music. Orchestral ensembles of wind and percussion instruments perform the musical parts. The vocal leader and the shamisen player conduct the narratives.

♦ THE ART OF PUPPET MANIPULATION
Three puppeteers are in charge of each puppet. This new technique dates back to 1734. The director, playwright, and master puppeteer, Monzaburo Yoshida, is its inventor. The chief manipulator handles the head and right arm of the puppet, the second moves the left arm, and the third one moves the legs.

♦ GIDAYU TAKEMOTO (1651–1714) In 1684, he founded the *Takemoto-za* theater in Osaka. He initiated an innovative style of dramatic narration for the puppet theater called *gidayu-bushi*. This style is still adopted in the *bunraku*. The *gidayu-bushi* needs a versatile interpreter gifted with vocal endurance, intonation, and melodramatic acting qualities.

♦ THE SHAMISEN Introduced in Japan in 1562, this three-stringed lute became the main accompaniment for the narrative (*joruri*). In the following century, it started to accompany the *joruri* even in the puppet theater.

♦ THE NOH MUSIC On a square wooden platform, topped with a roof, the two principal characters (*shite* and *waki*) sing songs in a rich and difficult language, while the chorus, aligned in two rows next to them, comment in unison upon the action. Behind the actors, there is the *hayashi,* the orchestral group composed of one bamboo flute (*nohkan*) and three drums of various sizes. They are the *O-tsuzumi* (hip drum) and the *Ko-tsuzumi* (shoulder drum) used to accompany dances and songs and the *taiko* (a barrel drum played with sticks). The last one is beaten only for dances. The flute accompanies dances and signals the beginning of a new section of the drama. This is the Noh, the most famous form of classical Japanese theater, created by the actors Kwan-Ami Kiyotsug (1333–1383) and his son, Zeami Motokiyo (1363–1444). It addresses the refined taste of the aristocratic class. Above, a mask from the Noh theater.

♦ THE NARRATOR He recites the dialogues of the puppets, narrates the events with a singing style similar to a sung recitative, and accompanies the performance with songs, when needed.

THE BUNRAKU Today, it designates the old genre of the puppet theater. Its essential elements are the charming musical way of narrating the stories, the music for *shamisen* (lute), and the fluid motions of the puppets. Warriors, aristocrats, and bourgeois are among the protagonists of the puppet theater.

THE DUKE'S COURT

In Europe, the slow transition from the Middle Ages to the modern era marked not only changes in genres, styles, and protagonists, but also a deep change in music's aim and values. Music continued to glorify God, but it asserted itself as an entertainment art too. Sovereigns and princes, now free from the church patronage, hired composers and musicians to cheer their evenings or to enhance their past and present dynastic glories. Moreover, ladies and noblemen listened and cultivated music as an undeniable part of their own education and personality enhancement.

♦ EUROPEAN COURTS
The Italian Renaissance courts of the sixteenth century or the French court of the seventeenth century were the most luminous examples of the engagement of political leaders in the promotion of culture and arts. Artists, poets, and even musicians enjoyed respect and economic support in the courts of European monarchs or princes. Moreover, they profited from a limited, but satisfying creative independence. The interest of the political party toward culture and arts responded to two objectives. The first was to create new values and ideals that justified and guided the behavior of the aristocracy, replacing the ascetic or warlike ideal. The second was to emphasize their authority and power to underline the growing supremacy of the monarchy. Above, F. Pourbous, *Ball at the Flanders Court.*

FAMOUS GUESTS
Toward the end of the sixteenth century, in his castle, Alfonso II, Duke of Ferrara, introduced his foreign guests to some of the principal musical attractions of the court of Este: the *gran concerto* and the *concerto delle dame.*

♦ CHORISTERS AND INSTRUMENTALISTS
The *gran concerto* of Ferrara was noted all over Europe for the exorbitant number of its choristers and instrumentalists. The number varied from 60 to 80 performers.

♦ THE THREE LADIES
The Ladies' Trio, formed by Laura Peperara, Tarquinia Molza, and Lucrezia Bendidio was celebrated all over Europe for the high level of its performances. An elaborate and difficult vocal style characterized their executions. Almost every evening, the trio performed in the private rooms of the Duchess.

♦ **ALFONSO II D'ESTE**
The Duke of Ferrara from 1559 to 1597, he always showed great consideration for his court musicians. He regarded them as the symbol of the wealth and power of his dominion.

♦ **THE RENAISSANCE**
The polyphony of the Flemish masters of the fifteenth century, built upon the superimposition of diverse melodies carried by various voices, led the way to the French chanson of the sixteenth century and to the Italian madrigal. It was still a polyphonic piece, but it emphasized harmony. It guarded that the superimposition of the different melodic lines did not produce disagreeable sounds. At the end of the sixteenth century, the monody became popular, which was a one-voice chant with instrumental accompaniment. It came from the polemics about polyphony, guilty of sacrificing the word to the music. The monodic chant was suited to theatrical representations and was at the origin of melodrama. Its success responded to the climate of rediscovery of classicism and the attempt of some Florentine poets to restore the ancient Greek tragedy. Above, a Renaissance lutist.

♦ **TORQUATO TASSO**
(1544–1595)
He was a poet at the Court of Este. His poems often were transposed into music. In his youth, he fell in love with Lucrezia Bendidio, whom he still looked upon with passion when he was older.

♦ **LUZZASCO LUZZASCHI**
(c.1540–1607)
Organist at the court of Alfonso II, he was one of the earliest examples of a professional musician. He was a popular author of madrigals, a polyphonic piece of three or more voices, which he composed for the Ladies' Trio.

♦ **A PAINTER**
A young court artist sketched the musical scene. Musical instruments and events can be depicted because music was now considered a noble activity.

THE SPANISH CONQUISTADORES

During the sixteenth century, the arrival of Spanish and Portuguese soldiers on the American continent upset the life of the natives. They suffered the systematic erosion of their culture and the forceful imposition of European culture and values. Music shared the same destiny. Colonies and missionaries forbade natives to perform their own music and dances, imposing instead Spanish and Portuguese melodies. They also introduced string instruments. In so doing, in Andean areas, the indigenous music disappeared or merged with European motifs, creating the *Mestizo* music. This type of music used European string instruments, local flutes (quena), and a mixture of native and European melodies.

♦ THE CONQUEST
The creation of the Spanish colonial empire in Central and South America is still bewildering. It is amazing how two Spanish adventurers, Hernán Cortés and Francisco Pizarro, during two different decades, were able to defeat the Aztec and Inca armies. In search of gold and with only a few hundred men, they created an empire that extended from Peru to Mexico. Their victories were not heroic exploits. They succeeded because they were ruthless, used explosive weapons, and profited from the internal differences splitting local populations. Cortés profited from the animosity of the populations conquered by the Aztecs. Pizarro profited from the internal dynastic conflicts that were eroding the Inca empire. He used them to crush the Incas between 1531 A.D. and 1533 A.D. Above, Cortés's portrait.

♦ MESTIZO MUSIC
The uniformity of the rhythm and the specific vocal style (a preference for the high register) reveal the native influence. Above, the Chilean group of the *Inti Illimani*.

MUSIC IN THE MISSIONS
After the conquest, music in the Catholic missions founded in Central and South America, accelerated the evangelization of the Indians.

♦ STRING INSTRUMENTS
Spanish and Portuguese colonialists brought string instruments to America. In Catholic missions, natives learned how to manufacture them.

42

NO FILES
Unfortunately, documents from the missions no longer exist. Consequently, no one is certain of the type of music performed and taught.

♦ JESUITS
A Jesuit accompanied the chant of a native with a guitar. The most recent traditional chants of Gregorian intonation demonstrate the changes undergone in the natives' music because of the Jesuit instruction.

♦ MEMORIES ON HOLD
Some Indian youth paint scenes on wood depicting the violent Spanish conquest. It is a desperate attempt at recording those tragic events.

JAVANESE SHADOW PUPPETS

Nestled in the Indonesian archipelago, the island of Java is the center of an ancient musical tradition that has its absolute protagonist in the gamelan. A gamelan is an orchestra composed mostly of gongs and metallophones, a few zithers and lutes, and three types of drums. Every village has a gamelan that plays during conciliatory and initiation rituals as well as during religious celebrations. Gamelan orchestras accompany almost all the musical and theatrical genres of the island, and especially the magic shadow theater. Spectators can appreciate an important element of the musical civilization of the area: the fusion of typical Far Eastern characters with Indian and Moslem traditions.

✦ **GONGS AND SONOROUS STONES**
The prevalence in the gamelan of gongs and sonorous stones and the use of the same instruments to execute melodic lines are typical characteristics of Far Eastern music.

FESTIVE NOTES
At the party for the circumcision of his son, a Javanese merchant has hired a gamelan to accompany the theatrical representation of a *Ramayana* episode. The shadow play began just before sunset and continued until 5:00 A.M. the next day.

✦ **REBAB**
Moslem domination during the sixteenth century increased the importance of string instruments and of the *rebab* (flute). The rebab led the melody as a solo instrument.

♦ ISLAM IN INDIA
AND IN SOUTHEAST
ASIA
A real conquest
followed the early
Islamic invasions
of India (eighth
century). At its
head, there was
the Sultan
Muhhamad of
Ghor (Governor
of the Arab
Empire of Turkish
origin). He
conquered the
Hindu kingdoms
of the north and
created, in 1206,
the Dehli
sultanate. The
Turkish domina-
tion continued
with vicissitude
until 1526. The
sultan showed
intolerance
toward the
Hindus. There
were frequent
conflicts between
Moslem lords and
farmers, loaded
down by too
many taxes.
Nonetheless, the
economy was
prosperous and
Indian and Arab
merchants
became wealthy.
The Indian
merchants, who,
during the first
century A.D., had
already diffused
Hinduism across
Indonesia, now
spread Islamism.
The archipelago
fell under Moslem
influence and, in
1515, Java was the
last Hindu reign
to succumb.
Above, an Islamic
building.

♦ PUPPETS
Made of leather,
richly decorated,
and having mobile
arms (since 1600),
they are an
ancient Indo-
nesian tradition.
The Hindu culture
influenced the
shadow theater,
which included
in its repertoire
the epic Indian
stories of the
Ramayana and
the *Mahabharata.*

♦ THE DALANG
He manipulated
all the figures,
produced sound
effects, narrated
and created the
story and gave
the starting signal
to musicians.

THE TEAHOUSE OPERA

The domination of the Mongolian dynasties and armies over the Chinese empire (1200) marked the passage from the refined art of court instrumental music to a theatrical form that Western countries eventually called opera. This is a synthesis of music, recitation, dance, and songs. Developed into a plurality of forms, the Chinese opera has been dominated for the last half century by the Peking style. Peking opera is a rich spectacle, based upon stories of emperors, concubines, and noble warriors, interpreted by skillful singer-actors. These talented performers have special vocal, mimic, and acrobatic skills. Built on rigid scenic and gestural rules, it alternates from recitation to singing and includes the intervention of an orchestra composed of percussion and string instruments.

IN THE TEAHOUSE
Half a century ago, in a Peking teahouse, where the rich merchants of the city met, a representation of the opera, *The Drunken Concubine,* was being performed.

✦ TANPI KU
It is a small drum resting on a stand. The tanpi ku player is the lead instrumentalist of the orchestra because he beats the tempo.

✦ HU CH'IN (ZITHER)
It is the most important string instrument, played mostly to accompany the melody tuned by the main character.

♦ GRACIOUS ACROBATICS
The concubine drank the wine in the cup and, with acrobatic move- ments, resulting from a long prepa- ration, she arched backward to place the cup on the tray behind her.

THE CONCUBINE
It is one of the six female roles, that of the young lover who is the opposite of the virtuous wife. She moves swiftly and has variable facial expressions. Boys interpreted feminine roles.

♦ THE HISTORY OF CHINA
Mongolian knights started to invade China in 1234. They conquered it in 1279. The Mongolian dynasties (1279–1368) opened China's frontiers to Western com- merce, but they failed to face the nationalistic revolts that gave the reins of the government to the Chinese Ming Dynasty. The Ming Dynasty (1368–1644) tenaciously resisted any foreign influence. Remarkable progress in manufacturing and the rise of a strong mercantile class marked this prosperous and progressive era. In 1644, China underwent another foreign domination, the Manchu. Manchu dynasties ruled until the arrival, during the nine- teenth century, of the Europeans, who forcibly imposed their economic interests. Above, the Mongol conqueror, Genghis Khan, in a Persian miniature from the fourteenth century.

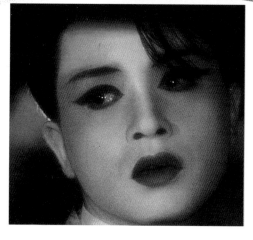

♦ TOUGH TRAINING
Reputed actors bought talented children from poor families to train them in the art of the Peking opera. Their methods were often inhuman. At left, a scene from the movie *Farewell, My Concubine* (1993).

♦ THE PUBLIC
In the midst of conversation, the public prefers the background of opera music, but a moderate sonorous volume and a predictable vocal style are expected.

GENIUS AND EXTRAVAGANCY

♦ CLASSICISM AND ROMANTICISM
Toward the end of the eighteenth century, European music faced some important novelties. The role of the musician changed. His public (the bourgeoisie) and the locales where he played his music (music chambers) changed. Even the musical genres changed. Instrumental music and Classicism, a new style made popular by Haydn and Mozart, predominated. Classicism regards a composition as a work where the single parts (movements, themes, and rhythms) oblige the ensemble to have mutual measure, balance, and strong reciprocal symmetries. Romanticism questioned the principles of the classical style. Instead of the symphonic cathedrals of Classicism, it preferred either the brief and intense expression of a *lieder* (a song for voice and piano) or the virtuoso exploits of a piano player. Above, Mozart's portrait.

For European musicians, the nineteenth century was delirious, but also difficult. It was delirious because music was no longer considered a simple vehicle of entertainment, but a true art, the creation from the minds of geniuses. It was difficult because with the end of the aristocratic patronage, musicians lost the economic safety that they derived from a stable position in the service of kings or princes. Finally free to compose at their whim, musicians were in reality forced to compromise with the taste of the larger bourgeois audiences, which guaranteed their survival through the purchase of printed scores.

♦ THE PIANO
A flexible instrument, with plenty of expressive possibilities, it became popular during the Romantic climate of the nineteenth century for the strong emphasis placed on individual feelings. Beethoven, Chopin, and Schumann were among the greatest piano interpreters. At left, Beethoven's piano.

♦ THE ORCHESTRA
Early in the nineteenth century, the orchestra disposed of an almost fixed layout with enriched tone color (all the instrument families were present) and an enlarged string section.

♦ HECTOR BERLIOZ (1803–1869) He was a French composer, univer- sally famous for his symphonic piece *Symphonie Fantastique.*

THE REHEARSAL OF A SYMPHONY
Berlioz, the French composer, was in Paris at the *Cirque Olympique* where he directed a concert almost a century and a half ago.

♦ THE *CIRQUE OLYMPIQUE*
It held more spectators than the other theaters. This choice was due to the greater demand for music from bourgeoisie and popular classes.

ART AND PUBLIC
Berlioz rehearsed some passages of a concerto in solitude. Artistic solitude was common to new composers, who in their increasingly original musical researches, detached themselves from the public.

♦ THE STRING QUARTET
During the nineteenth century, the quartet found its best expression in German venues thanks to masterpieces by Beethoven, Schumann, and Brahms. Above, Haydn directs a string quartet.

49

UPRISING AND SAMBA

Forced to leave their homelands, thousands of Africans were sold as slaves to South American landowners to work in tobacco or sugar cane fields. Their history includes the fight for the recognition of their dignity and the fiery battle to assert their culture and identity. Often hiding themselves, African slaves built drums with which they reproduced the frenetic rhythms of their native lands. With them, they accompanied fast and syncopated dances of mysterious and magic meaning. Slower and smoother, the same rhythms passed into the samba, a dance and type of music symbolic of Brazil. The samba is the definitive African contribution to South American music.

♦ LATIN AMERICA IS FREE!
The end of Spanish and Portuguese rule over Latin America was ignited by Creole uprisings, not by native or slave revolts. Creoles were white and born in the colonies. They were privileged members of colonial society. National revolts exploded during the early years of the nineteenth century. The Venezuelan, Simón Bolivar (1783–1830) and Argentinean, José de San Martín (1778–1850) excelled as commanders of these revolts. Latin America did not join in a confederation, like the North American states did, disappointing many. Latin America broke into several sovereign states. It remained fragmented politically and even socially with, on one side, the Creoles in charge of the political power and riches, and, on the other, the oppressed and overworked natives and blacks. Above, Simón Bolivar's portrait.

♦ BATUCADA AND MAGIC
Forced to convert to Christianity, slaves secretly tried to recreate their ancient cults. With its pulsating rhythms, the *batucada* drags dancers into trances, an ideal condition for communicating with benevolent spirits.

♦ DRUMS
Batucada's typical instruments are drums of various sizes and the *agogô,* a double cowbell instrument struck with a stick, which has its roots in African music.

IN THE STREETS OF RIO
At the end of the last century, former African slaves fled to Rio and erected barricades along the streets. They claimed the right to amuse themselves with dances and music. Slavery ended in Brazil in 1888.

BATUCADA
Former slaves loosen up in a frenetic *batucada* (dances and music brought to South America by African slaves). *Batucada* always has very fast rhythms and the obsessive accompaniment of percussion instruments.

✦ CARIBBEAN RHYTHMS
In Central America, the presence of black slaves explains a type of music undoubtedly African in its characteristics, which consisted of syncopated rhythms, the use of drums, and the typical chant that alternated between the soloist and chorus. This music merged with another one in vogue: the music of Spanish origin, marked by a melodic trait and the abundance of string instruments. Rumba and mambo, two ballroom dances, originated from this. They are both exuberant dances, built on the crossing of fast rhythms, accompanied by guitars. By becoming a ballroom dance, the rumba lost its magic origin, becoming a courting dance. Central American dances are acclaimed worldwide. They have influenced jazz and rock and roll. Above, Tito Puente and his orchestra in 1960.

✦ THE SLAVES
The African slave markets in the South American colonies began during the first decades of the sixteenth century, when it became clear that the natives would not bear the inhuman work in the fields and mines.

GYPSY MUSIC

Europe has a diverse panorama of popular music. It is a music composed, performed, and listened to by even the humblest strata of the population. It is very difficult for this reason to find a common thread linking the Swiss yodel, Finnish epic chants, and German work songs. Often however, one finds amazing sonorous similarities among popular traditions thousands of miles apart. In Moscow, for instance, one can listen to notes echoing the popular music of Granada. One explanation may lie in a common gypsy source. Always traveling across Europe, Tzigane musicians would be responsible for the mixing and exchanges between distant musical traditions.

♦ **IRISH MUSIC**
Unlike most of Europe, Irish popular music is not a historical finding that pedantic researchers can investigate by piling up interviews with octogenarians. It is a very energetic type of music. At the classic Anglo-Irish meeting points, in the pubs, between beers, both young and old sing yearning ballads (songs with a limited number of strophes); songs crowded with love and heroes. In the same pubs, small bands still perform, following an important instrumental musical tradition: a wooden flute, a frame drum, and a whistle. These performers are skillful improvisers. Dance music is also very popular. Its most ancient form is the jig (*gigue*), a dance in fast and triple time. Above, an Irish folk scene.

♦ **POPULAR MUSICIANS**
Local musicians listen with a flicker of curiosity. No one is sure who is the true inspirational source of Gypsy music: the Tziganes or the provincial musicians who became fascinated by Gypsy musical styles and forms.

♦ **THE MARRIED COUPLE**
The wedding is celebrated with a special rite not requiring the presence of a pastor.

FROM ALL OVER EUROPE

In a Ukrainian village at the end of the nineteenth century, a wedding party was going on. For the occasion, relatives of the various Gypsy communities have arrived from all corners of Europe.

♦ FLAMENCO
Spanish Tziganes dance a feverish flamenco, a type of dance and chant flavored with Gypsy music and Andalusian chants.

♦ YIDDISH MUSIC
It is the musical tradition of Jewish communities across Central and Eastern Europe. Their language was Yiddish, a mix of German, Hebrew, and Neo-Latin words. A popular music performed in ghettos, it was reinvigorated by mystical Jewish trends spread during the seventeenth century. Their criticism of the traditional interpretation of the Bible as well as of the liturgy performed in the synagogues, promoted freer instrumental expressions, able to inspire prophetic visions. Later words punctuated the repertoire, styliz-ing the realistic and magic worlds that characterized the Jewish communities of Eastern Europe. Yiddish music is a hybrid between popular Eastern European traditions (Russian, Hungarian, Romanian, and German) and Middle-Eastern music. Above, *Geigenspieler,* by Marc Chagall, 1920.

♦ THE VIOLIN
It is the soul of Gypsy music. It is always present in many legends that narrate its marvelous origin.

♦ TZIGANE VIOLINISTS
There is also the Hungarian Gypsy community. Both its violinists and music (called Tzigane), rhyth-mic and full of virtuosity, are known across Europe. They have both influ-enced cultivated musicians like Liszt.

♦ BÉLA BARTÓK
(1881–1945). This Hungarian compos-er was the author of many remarkable studies in ethnomusicology. He showed great interest for popular music, which he tried to merge with the more modern cultivated music.

AFRICAN-AMERICAN MUSIC

The United States has offered some of the richest and newest musical experiences of the twentieth century: blues, jazz, and lately, rap. These three musical genres share the same African origin, recognizable by the vocal style of the blues, the extemporaneity of jazz, and the rhythms of rap. Oppressed by slavery and secluded for a long time from education, African-Americans have found in music the simplest and most natural way to assert their identities and express their world and experiences.

♦ **CHANTS**
African-American soldiers sing, in their typical African scheme of call and response, the chants of slavery as sung in the cotton and tobacco fields. These chants are the oldest musical form of the African-American community and the source of blues and jazz.

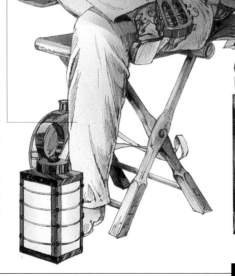

♦ **JAZZ MUSIC**
It has Charlie Parker (at left), Louis Armstrong, Duke Ellington, and Dizzie Gillespie among its protagonists as well as many experiences from New Orleans to swing, and from bop to cool jazz.

♦ **THE CREOLES**
In North America, the word *Creoles* refers to people born out of mixed unions, where one of the parents is black and the other is white. The Creoles mediated the exchanges between African and European music. Because of them, some string instruments entered into the African-American repertoire.

♦ **RAP**
It is a series of rhythmical strophes on a prerecorded musical basis. Born in the ghettos, it reflects the language, hopes, and rage felt by African-Americans. Left, *Public Enemy,* American rap band.

A MOMENT OF RELAXATION
One evening in 1864, at the front when the Civil War was almost over, a battalion of African-Americans take a break from their harsh daily duties.

♦ THE BIBLE
Bible stories and the Passion of Christ (a clear reference to the tormented life of the slaves) are themes of the gospel, religious chants of the African-American community.

♦ THE CIVIL WAR
(1861–1865)
The United States is a Federal state with a central government that deals with foreign politics, defense, and national economy. Each state has the power to decide on education, justice, taxes, and local police. Around the first half of the nineteenth century, northern and southern states had opposing views on slavery. The North wanted to abolish slavery, while the South, mostly for economic reasons (landowners needed slaves to farm their lands), wanted it retained. Moreover, the South threatened to leave the Union. Upon the election of President Abraham Lincoln (1809–1865), the southern states decided to dissociate themselves from the Union (1860) and form a confederacy. Lincoln declared war on the Confederacy, winning in 1865. Above, Abraham Lincoln's portrait.

♦ THE BLUES
It is an African-American solo singing veined with solitude and melancholy. Bessie Smith (left) and Billie Holiday excel for the emotional intensity of their voices.

♦ THE RHYTHM
A soldier beats the tempo. One of the greatest gifts of the African-American community to

North American music is the emphasis on rhythmic aspects, particularly evident in jazz.

TANGO

During this century's early years, in the suburbs of Buenos Aires, a fiery, desperate, and colorful mix of Italians, Spanish, African, and Creole immigrants invented a music and a dance that were sentimental, sometimes erotic, and always melancholic. It is the Argentinean tango, a fusion of Caribbean and African-American rhythms (*batucada*), of Andalusian music, Italian melodies, and especially of the Argentinean *payada* (the typical song of the *gaucho*). In an unresolved contrast between fast rhythm and slow melody, the tango as a dance is the representation of a perennial and desperate duel between man and woman or between the immigrant (male dancer) and Argentina (female dancer).

♦ **THE HISTORY OF TANGO**
Born in the ill-reputed districts of Buenos Aires, the tango soon moved to bourgeois salons and theaters. From Argentina, it went to Paris and London, passing through the United States. In Europe, some steps were judged too erotic and were altered. The strong hold of the male dancer on the female dancer loosened up a little. In spite of the lingering suspicions of indecency, the tango gained a universal success. In 1914, some diplomats were accused of dancing the tango inside the Argentinean embassy, which caused a clamor. Among the fathers of tango, there was the French immigrant Carlos Gardel (1890–1935), who abandoned the swift rhythms for the slow and melancholic melodies. When he died, Astor Piazzolla (1921–1992) renewed the tango. Above, Carlos Gardel's poster.

♦ **THE *COMPADRE***
One of the tango's earlier figures is the former *gaucho* (the cowboy of the pampas), who arrived in Buenos Aires for employment. He has sideburns, hair pasted with gel, and flashy outfits. He survives using tricks of all kinds. He is quarrelsome and behaves as the quarter's bully.

♦ **IMMIGRANTS**
The tango is the expression of the immigrant's nostalgia, the burning memory of the homeland, and the frustration of present miseries.

♦ **THE HARBOR**
Originally, the tango was close to the rhythms of *habanera,* an Afro-Cuban dance, which probably landed in Buenos Aires with seamen sailing to the Caribbean islands.

♦ **THE STAB**
The tango is a simulation of a fight or a duel, with attacks and defensive movements. It is one of the reasons why men can tango by themselves.

♦ **THE BORDELLO**
Once, the tango was mostly played in brothels. It was the music of prostitutes and bad guys and focused on betrayed and illicit love.

♦ **RUDOLF VALENTINO**
Rudolf Valentino, a star of silent films, by performing as a questionable *gaucho,* contributed to tango's popularity.

A MURDER
Near the Buenos Aires harbor, a young *compadre* kills a *gaucho* who has come to town.

♦ **BANDONEON**
It is the soul of tango. Invented around 1860 by the German, Heinrich Band, it is a type of concertina with a melancholic and dramatic sound.

TAKEOVER OF WEI-HU MOUNTAIN

In the twentieth century, technology, lifestyles, culture, and Western music have exerted a strong and lasting impression on other world's civilizations. All musical cultures, from the cultivated Arabian to the popular African, have tried to acculturate Western music. Even the Chinese opera has welcomed Western theatrical and musical models. Actors are not responsible for this choice. The Chinese Communist party has attempted to slowly erase previous culture and tradition by training people to accept new values.

♦ THE REGIME AND THE CHINESE OPERA
The attitude of the Chinese Communist party toward the traditional Chinese opera was ambiguous. It was supportive and considered it a popular and national form of art, but it also criticized its values and conventions. The leaders of the Chinese People's Republic reproached the traditional opera for the importance given to aristocrats, the marginal role reserved for common workers, and the splendor of the costumes. Therefore, it renewed traditional opera. It was like making new buds blossom from an old tree: modern stories (life in the country or episodes of national heroic wars), the abolition of submissive behaviors (bowing), and the use of everyday costumes. Actors received a different training, including a ban on corporal punishment of undisciplined apprentices. Above, Peking Opera.

THE OPERA
In the theater of the Peking Opera (1969), the model play *Takeover of Wei-Hu Mountain* is on stage. In the first scene, a detachment of the Chinese People's Republican Army advances through the snow.

♦ SU YANG
He is the hero of the opera. He is singing a song. In the new Chinese opera, singing prevails over music and dance, because words have to carry the more important political and educational message.

♦ ORCHESTRA
The Communist party, which exercises a strict control over the liberal arts, dictates that an orchestra must simultaneously display both traditional and Western instruments.

♦ **The new opera**
Chinese opera's repertoire and themes changed with the Communist Revolution. Workers and soldiers replaced emperors and concubines, which were remnants of a feudal epoch.

♦ **Mao Tse-tung**
He was the leader of the Chinese Communist party.

♦ **Chinese Revolution**
In 1911, a popular uprising swept over the Chinese empire, bringing the proclamation of the republic. The maneuvers and power of the military forces soon weakened the republic. Corrupt and inept, the bourgeoisie revolted, represented by the Kuomintang party, as well as the workers led by the Communist party. In a fragile alliance, these forces defeated the warlords. The Kuomintang, however, tried to rid itself of the communists who had proposed the agricultural reform. In response, Mao Tse-tung, their leader, gathered together his men and, between 1934 and 1935, reached the safe regions of the north and counterattacked. After a common war against Japan, the Kuomintang and the revolutionary forces continued to fight each other. Mao Tse-tung won and proclaimed the Chinese People's Republic in 1949. Above, Mao Tse-tung.

♦ **Western instruments**
They are mostly string instruments, used to create an epic atmosphere during war scenes.

ROCK AND ROLL

THE CONCERT
U2 in concert in the 1980s.
World concert tours are one of rock's most important achievements.

In the United States, during the first half of the fifties, rock and roll ignited a revolution in Western popular music. Dominated until then by romantic and melodic songs with clear and limpid voices, popular music ceded to frenetic rhythms, growling, and often wailing voices. The behavior and attitudes of singers changed. They became more irreverent, teasing, and explicitly sensual. Audiences changed too. During the course of their performances, they started to move, sing, and shout. Rock offers the first example of music written for one generation: the youth. Parents and children stopped listening to the same type of music.

♦ THE HISTORY
OF ROCK
Rock and roll comes from the fusion of black rhythm and blues with white country music. Its precursor was Bill Haley, with his prolonged impromptu with the guitar. Nevertheless, it was Elvis Presley who embodied rock's soul. He was the first star of rock, unforgettable with his frenetic and sensual movements. Early rock changed during the sixties due to the English beat. The sound and even the role of the amplified electric guitar became predominant. Legendary groups such as the Beatles and the Rolling Stones caused this transformation. Folk music with Bob Dylan and soul music with James Brown and other black artists departed from the beat. From the 1970s on, rock has broken up into a series of genres and subgenres, from punk to hard rock, from folk rock to soft rock. Above, Elvis Presley.

♦ DRUMS
It is a percussion instrument, which stressed one of the important aspects of rock: rhythm.

♦ U2
Today, along with R.E.M, it is one of the most popular rock groups on earth. Of Irish origin, they have blended rhythmic rock and Irish ballads.

♦ THE ELECTRIC GUITAR

More than a rhythmic revolution, rock has been a revolution of sounds and their combinations. The timbre of the amplified electric guitar was absolutely new.

♦ THE PUBLIC

Unlike folk music, rock always separates performers from listeners. However, unlike cultivated music, the public does not only evaluate the performance with, for example, a final clapping, but rather participates during the event by moving and singing.

♦ CULTIVATED MUSIC OF THE TWENTIETH CENTURY

The Romantics had already stated that music was a universal art, free from the tastes of the general public as well as from the ties of score buyers. During the twentieth century, this statement strengthens and originates the phenomenon of the avant-garde. The composer refuses any language linked to forms and styles of the tradition and works at creating an absolutely new music. The experiences of Arnold Schöenberg, Anton Webern, and Alban Berg are inspired by this principle. They are among the most remarkable composers of the twentieth century. Avant-garde, however, changes the relationship between public and composer. If Western popular music attracted a packed crowd, cultivated music tended to separate itself from the public, becoming comprehensible only to well-trained ears. Above, Alban Berg.

WORLD MUSIC

New and improved means of transportation have shortened distances, changed the world's view, and brought cultures together. This is true for music, too. One can now turn on a Western radio and listen to Algerian *raï* or Jamaican *reggae*. Cultural exchanges are frequent and people generally do not remain isolated in their own traditions. They enjoy mixing styles, different forms of composition, timbres, and instruments from diverse and far away musical civilizations. In so doing, they explore new territories and renew traditions that, because of the supremacy of Western pop music, might disappear forever.

♦ NUSRAT FATH ALI KHAN
(1948–1997)
His father, a musician, wished he became a doctor, but Nusrat always cultivated his passion and love for *qawwali,* the ancient repertoire of mystic Moslem music and chant (Sufi). *Qawwali* is a devotional music, whose vocal style rests on bold and powerful virtuosisms.

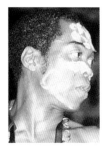

♦ FELA ANIKULAPO KUTI
(1938–1997)
Persecuted by the authorities of his native country, Nigeria, for denouncing the violation of political and civil rights, he was one of the few African musicians to reach worldwide popularity. His music blended traditional African rhythms with modern Western sounds.

AMONG FRIENDS
In the *Real World* studios, the record house founded by Peter Gabriel in Bath, England, a few friends, true heroes of the world music, are gathered.

♦ TRIO BULGARKA
This trio has rewritten traditional Bulgarian music to meet Western tastes.

♦ PETER GABRIEL
Once, he was leader of *Genesis,* the famous rock group. Now, as a soloist, he is one of the most creative champions of world music and an active supporter with his record house.

♦ YOSSU'N DOUR
Senegalese, he is the son of an African *griot* (a professional entertainer) from whom he has inherited warm vocal tones. He is a star of international and African music.

♦ PAPA WEMBA
He is an original Congolese musician who knows how to mix his homeland traditional music with Caribbean rhythms and rhythm and blues.

♦ **CHEB KALED**
King of the renewed Algerian *raï,* a popular music of a sometimes scabrous subject that celebrates joy of living and carnal pleasures. For these themes, he has been hated by the most violent Islamic devotees.

♦ **SAKAMOTO**
He has successfully mixed Western music and Japanese traditional music. He has written important movie tracks, among which include *The Last Emperor.*

♦ **RAVI SHANKAR**
Performer of Indian traditional music, he is known worldwide for some of his works with Western musicians.

♦ **UNUSUAL UNIONS**
One of the most vital characteristics of recent world music is the research of new sounds through the superimposition and union of instruments belonging to past or far away civilizations with modern instruments.

INDEX